The Mickey Mouse

Library of Congress Cataloging in Publication Data
The Mickey Mouse make-it book.
(Disney's wonderful world of reading, #21)
Easy-to-read, step-by-step instructions for ten things to make and do with rubber bands, soda pop cans, aluminum foil, crayons, scissors and other common items.
1. Handicraft–Juvenile literature. [1. Handicraft]   TT160.M47   745.5   74-5241   ISBN 0-394-82555-1
ISBN 0-394-92555-6 (lib. bdg.)
Manufactured in the United States of America
E F G H I J K
4   5   6   7   8   9

BOOK CLUB EDITION

MAKE-IT
BOOK

Random House 🏠 New York

A Note
From Mickey

Dear Girls and Boys,

Here is a book of things you can make.

It is a special kind of activity book because you can read it yourself!

The pictures will help, too.

But that's not all!

The things you need are easy to find.

Each step is easy to do.

Best of all, after you make these things you can have fun playing with them.

So have a good time!

Love,

Mickey

Mickey Mouse Puppet

You can make your own Mickey Mouse puppet.

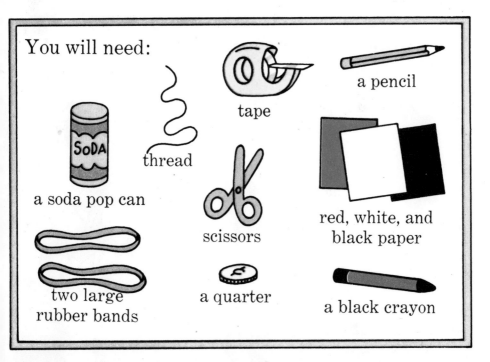

You will need:

tape

a pencil

thread

a soda pop can

scissors

red, white, and black paper

two large rubber bands

a quarter

a black crayon

1   Draw around a soda pop can to make
one circle on red paper,
one circle on white paper,
and two circles on black paper.

2   Draw around a quarter
to make four circles
on white paper.

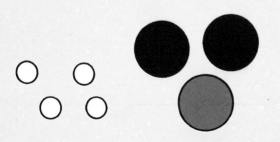

3   Cut out all the circles.

4 Draw Mickey's face on the large white circle.

5 Color in Mickey's eyes and nose.

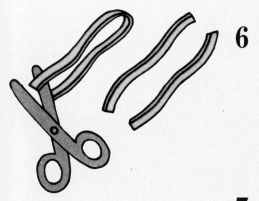

6 Cut each rubber band in half.

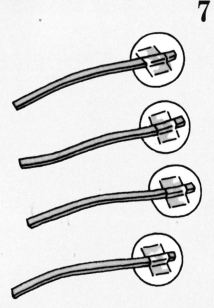

7 Tape one piece of rubber band to each small white circle.

These are Mickey's arms and legs.

8 Tape the two black circles to the top of Mickey's head

These are Mickey's ears.

9 Tape the ears down in back, too.

10 Tape the red circle under Mickey's chin.

This is Mickey's body.

11 Tape the body down in back.

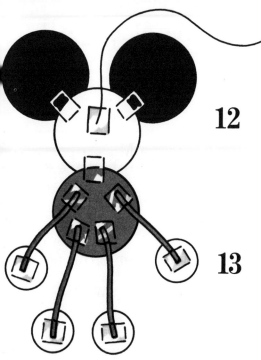

12 Tape a piece of thread to the back of his head.

13 Tape Mickey's arms and legs to the back of his body.

To make Mickey dance, just move the thread up and down.
Watch his arms and legs jiggle!

Wacky Ball

This ball bounces in a wacky way. If you save lots of rubber bands— which is a wacky thing to do— you can make a Wacky Ball.

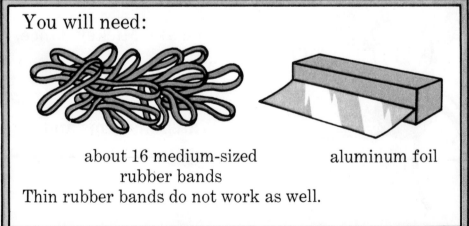

You will need:

about 16 medium-sized rubber bands

aluminum foil

Thin rubber bands do not work as well.

1 Tear off a piece of foil about the size of this page.

2 Crumple it up into a ball.

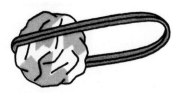

3 Put a rubber band around the ball.

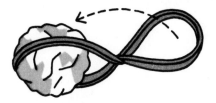

4 Twist it and put it around again.

5 Wrap more rubber bands around the ball.

6 Cover up the foil as much as possible.

Now bounce the ball. But watch out!

The Lost Shadow

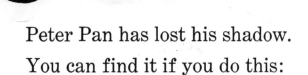

Peter Pan has lost his shadow.
You can find it if you do this:

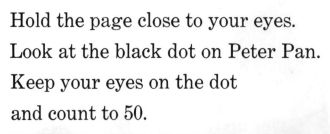

Hold the page close to your eyes.
Look at the black dot on Peter Pan.
Keep your eyes on the dot
and count to 50.
Look at a wall and blink your eyes.
Is that Peter's shadow on the wall?

Captain Hook Bank

Captain Hook knows a good place to hide his money. He puts it in his bank.

You will need:

a pencil

red, white, and black paper

scissors

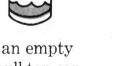

an empty pull top can

tape

a black crayon

a saucer

Hook's Head

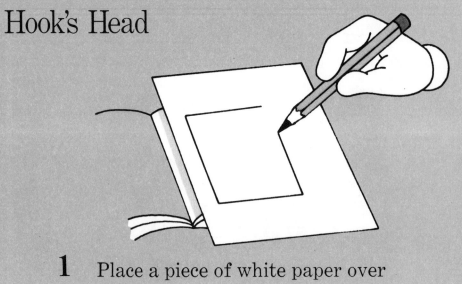

1 Place a piece of white paper over the rectangle on the next page.

2 Trace around the rectangle.

3 Trace the eyes and the moustache with a black crayon.

This is Captain Hook's face.

This is for tracing.

4 Cut out the rectangle that you traced.

5 Wrap it around the pull top can.

6 Tape the paper together at the back.

The hole in the can should be at the top.

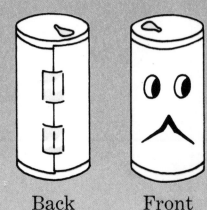

Back   Front

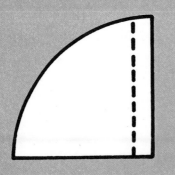

This is for
tracing.

7 Place a piece of
white paper over
the shape at the
top of this page.

8 Trace around
the shape.

9 Trace the broken line.

10 Cut out the shape
that you traced.

This shape will
be a pattern.

11 Place the shape
on red paper and
draw around it.

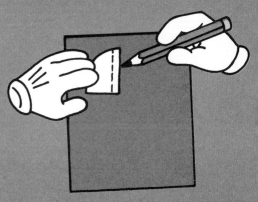

12 Cut out the red shape.

This is Hook's nose.

13 Draw the broken line
on it.

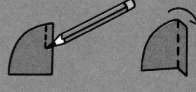

14 Fold the nose
on the broken line.

15 Tape the nose
to Hook's face.

Hook's Hair

1 Cut out six strips of black paper.

Each strip should be about this size.

2 Roll the end of each strip around a pencil.

The strips are Hook's hair.

3 Tape Hook's hair to the back of Hook's head.

Hook's Hat

1 Draw around
a saucer
to make a circle
on red paper.

2 Cut out the circle.

3 Place Hook's head
in the middle of the
red circle.

4 Draw around it.

5 Cut out the circle in the middle of the circle.

6 Fold up the sides of the red circle.

This is for tracing.

7   Place a piece of white paper over the shape at the top of this page.

8   Trace around the shape.

9   Cut out the shape that you traced.

This is a feather for Hook's hat.

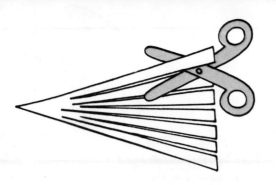

10 Cut toward the point to make thin strips.

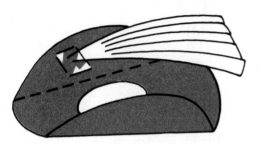

11 Tape the point of the feather to one side of the hat.

12 Put the hat on Hook's head.

13 Tape the hat to the can.

Now fill your Captain Hook Bank with coins.
When it is full, open it with a can opener.

Magic Letters

What does Dumbo's sign say?
To find out, do this:
Close one eye.
Hold the book flat
up to your other eye.

Now read Dumbo's sign.

Flappy Dumbo

The ears on this toy Dumbo flap
just like the ears on the real Dumbo.

You will need:

a piece of paper

a plastic straw

a crayon

tape

scissors

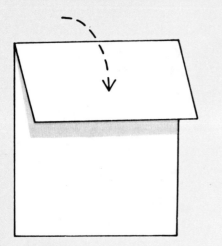

1 Fold the paper into three equal parts.

Fold down the top.

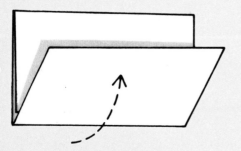

Fold up the bottom.

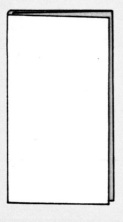

2 Turn the paper so that it looks like this.

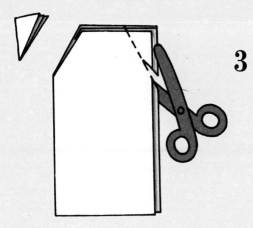

3 Cut off two
small corners
at the top.

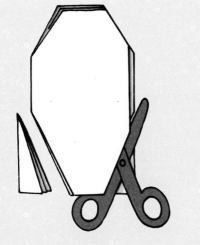

4 Cut off two
long corners
at the bottom.

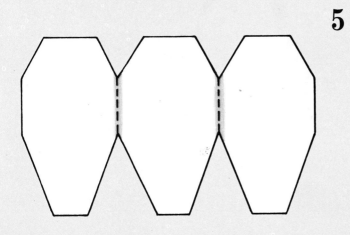

5 Open up
the paper.

This is
Dumbo.

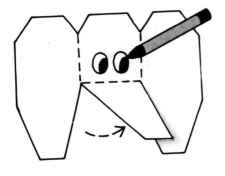

6 Draw the eyes on Dumbo's face.

7 Fold up Dumbo's trunk.

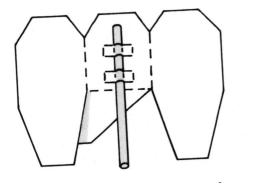

8 Tape the straw to the back of Dumbo's head.

Hold the end of the straw.
Move Dumbo back
and forth slowly.
Do his ears flap?

Paper Parrot

Every pirate should have a parrot.
Smee has a parrot that never talks back
and doesn't cost money to feed.

You will need:

a pencil

colored paper scraps
(including green)

a soda pop can

a black crayon

tape

scissors

1 Place the tape holder down on green paper.

2 Draw around it.

If your tape holder does not make this shape, draw it by yourself!

3 Cut out the shape that you drew.

This is the head of the parrot.

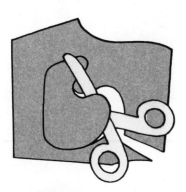

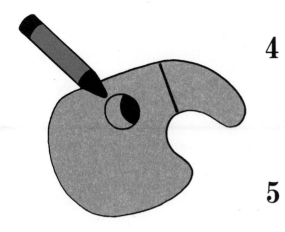

4 Draw a line
on both sides
for the beak.

5 Draw an eye
on both sides.

6 Draw around a
soda pop can
to make a circle
on colored paper.

7 Cut out the circle.

This is the body
of the parrot.

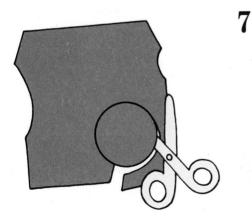

8 Tape the head
to the body on
both sides.

9 Cut out three
strips of colored
paper to make
the feathers.

Each strip should
be about this size.

10 Tape the feathers
on the parrot.

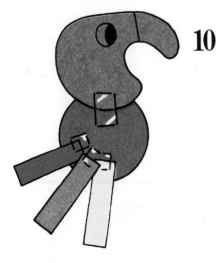

Your Paper Parrot will look
great hanging on your wall!

Goofy Wheels

Goofy never has to buy any gas.

His car runs by magic.

Look at the wheels.

Move the book around in small circles.

See the wheels turn!

Huey's Balancing Toy

This toy keeps its balance—
just like Huey.
Make one and see for yourself!

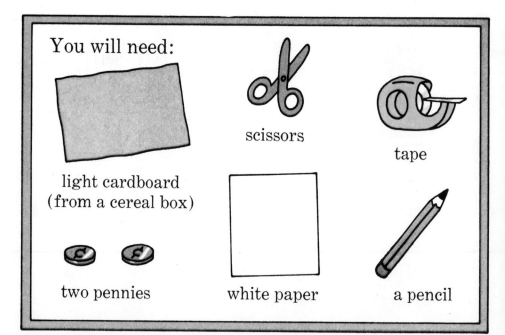

You will need:

light cardboard
(from a cereal box)

scissors

tape

two pennies

white paper

a pencil

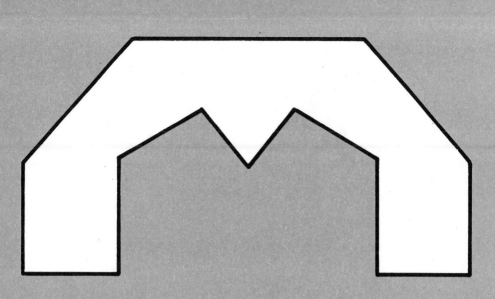

This is for tracing.

1 Place a piece of white paper over the shape at the top of this page.

2 Trace around the shape.

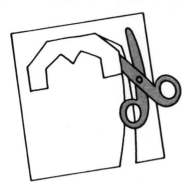

3 Cut out the shape that you traced.

4 Place the shape on light cardboard and draw around it.

5 Cut out the shape that you drew on the cardboard.

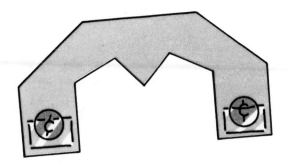

6 Tape two pennies to the bottom of the shape— one on each end.

Now try to balance this toy on your finger.

Spin it around on the end of a glass.

It will balance on almost anything!

The Twirly Whirly

Here is a toy that twirls and whirls as it
falls to the ground—just like a helicopter!

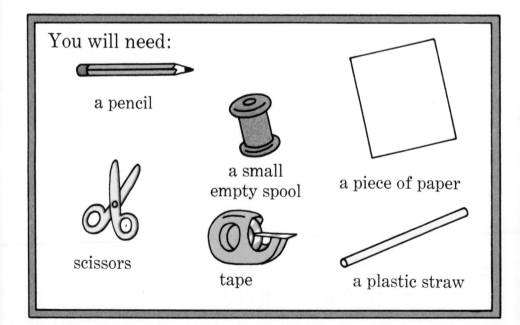

You will need:

a pencil

a small
empty spool

a piece of paper

scissors

tape

a plastic straw

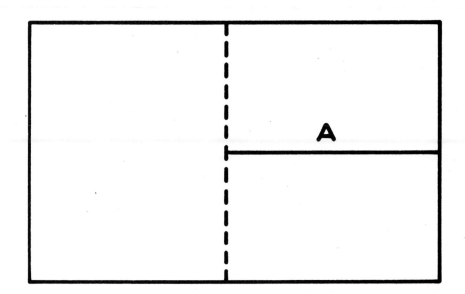

This is for tracing.

1   Place a piece of white paper over the rectangle at the top of this page.

2   Trace the rectangle, Line A, and the broken line.

3 Cut out the rectangle that you traced.

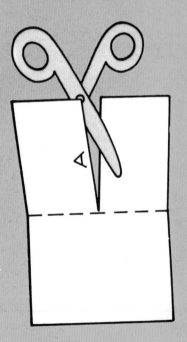

4 Cut along Line A to make two flaps.

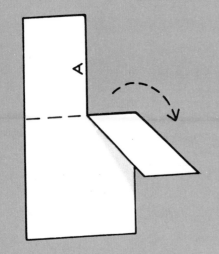

5 Fold one flap forward on the broken line.

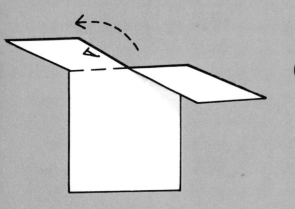

6 Fold one flap backward on the broken line.

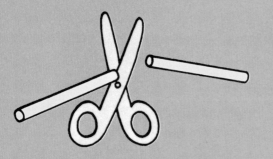

7 Cut a straw in half.

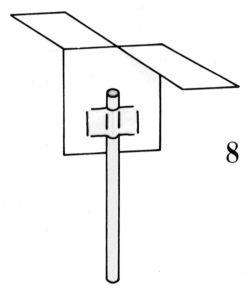

8 Tape one half of the straw to the paper below the flaps.

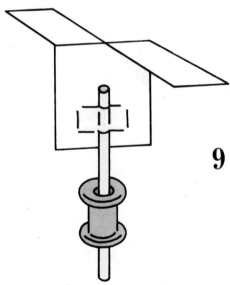

9 Put the straw through the empty spool.

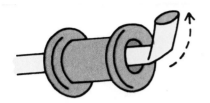

10 Fold up a small piece of the straw at the end.

11 Tape it down to the spool.

This is how the toy looks when it is done.

Now throw it up in the air.
Watch it whirl as it falls!
The higher you throw it,
the better the action!